Exploring
the Everglades

Andrew Collins

Contents

United States

Florida

Everglades

A Wet Wilderness

There's no other place in the world like the Everglades. There's a lot to see and do in this huge **wilderness area** in southern Florida. You can hike through a cypress swamp. You can ride a bike through the saw grass. You can take a boat tour around many islands. Come on, let's go!

The Everglades is a **wetland**. That means the ground is often soaked with water. The amount of water changes with the seasons.

There are only two seasons in the Everglades. During the wet season, rain fills up the Everglades. The Everglades becomes a wide, grassy river. In the dry season, much of the water dries up. Plants and animals must be able to survive in both seasons.

Wet season

Dry season

There are many wetland **habitats** within the Everglades. Each habitat is home to special plants and animals. We'll visit three wetland habitats on our trip.

Let's keep track of the different kinds of plants and animals we see as we tour the Everglades. Every time we see something new, we'll put a mark on our tally sheet.

Tally Sheet

Mammals
Birds
Reptiles
Shellfish
Fish
Insects
Plants

Hiking Through a Swamp

Our journey begins in the northwest corner of the Everglades. This part of the Everglades is a **swamp** habitat. Swamps have soft, wet ground and still water.

The best way to explore here is on foot. That means getting wet. We put on long pants and old sneakers. Then we step into the dark, muddy water.

A forest of cypress trees grows in the swamp. Cypress trees are a kind of tree that can grow in standing water. You can see the roots of the cypress tree in the soft, wet ground.

Cypress tr

Looking up into the trees we see a strange sight. It looks like the tree is growing hair. It is really Spanish moss. Spanish moss is a kind of plant that grows without soil.

Spanish moss

We use nets to find small animals in the water. Look at this crayfish. It looks like a little lobster. We put the crayfish back in the water after we look at it.

As we walk along, we see a turtle lying in the sun on a rock. Most turtles have hard shells on their backs to protect them from **predators**. This turtle has a pattern on its legs and head that helps hide the turtle when it swims.

Crayfish

Let's tally up the plants and animals we saw today. We saw a crayfish, which is a type of shellfish. We saw a turtle, which is a reptile. We also saw plants we've never seen before. We saw cypress trees and Spanish moss.

Tally Sheet

Mammals	
Birds	
Reptiles	
Shellfish	I
Fish	I
Insects	
Plants	II

Biking with Birds

Today, we're going to ride bikes along a path in Everglades National Park. The Everglades is often referred to as a river of grass, and now we know why. Tall saw grass grows as far as you can see.

In the wet season, the ground here is covered in shallow water. In the dry season, there is less water, but the soil is still muddy. This habitat is called a **marsh**. A marsh is wet like a swamp, but the water is deeper and it flows.

As we ride along, the first thing we see is a tall, white bird walking through the shallow water. It is a snowy egret. The bird quickly sticks its long beak into the water and comes up with a fish.

Snowy egret

We see lots of small trees growing along the edge of the water. These are called palmetto trees. Animals like to hide in the palmetto trees. When we look closely, we see a rough green snake. This snake can climb trees. It can swim, too.

Rough green snake

Later, we use our binoculars to see several pink and white birds. They are tall and they have beaks shaped like spoons. These birds are called roseate spoonbills. They use their spoon-shaped beaks to search for fish to eat.

Roseate spoonbills

We look down at the water to see if we can find some fish. We spot some little fish that are no bigger than our thumbs. They are called killifish. Most fish lay eggs, but the killifish doesn't. It has one baby fish at a time.

Killifish

There are some areas of dry land within the marsh. These areas are called **hammocks**. A hammock is like a small island. Trees grow thickly on the hammocks. The air is damp. It's the perfect habitat for flowers like orchids.

Orchid

Otter

The hammocks provide a home for many animals. Otters are a kind of mammal. They make their homes in old logs or in river banks. They swim in the water and catch fish to eat.

We stare for a long time at something on the river bank that looks like rough rocks. Finally, the "rocks" move! It is an alligator resting in the sun. Many alligators live in the Everglades.

Let's tally up what we saw today. We saw several plants. We saw orchids, saw grass, and palmetto trees. We saw two kinds of birds. We saw a snowy egret and roseate spoonbills. We saw fish called killifish. We saw an alligator and a snake, which are both reptiles. Finally, we saw an otter, which is a mammal.

Tally Sheet

Mammals	I
Birds	II
Reptiles	III
Shellfish	I
Fish	I
Insects	
Plants	IIII

Touring the Islands

Our last stop is in a part of the Everglades known as Ten Thousand Islands. Most of the islands are small and covered with trees. We explore this part of the Everglades by boat. At times, the stretch of water is wide. At other times, it is quite narrow.

Fresh water and sea water mix in this part of the Everglades. Mangrove trees grow here. They can grow in salty water. They have roots that stick out of the water like stilts.

Mangrove trees

Many kinds of birds live in this part of the Everglades. Suddenly, a large bird dives down into the water. It is an osprey. It catches a fish with its feet. We sit quietly and watch the bird fly away with its fish.

As we sit still, a long skinny insect lands nearby. It has four long wings that glitter in the sunlight. It is a dragonfly.

Dragonfly

We see an animal the size of a cow up ahead in the water. It's a manatee. A manatee is a kind of mammal that lives in the water here. We are lucky to see a manatee. They are very shy animals.

Manat

Let's add the plants and animals we saw today to our tally. We saw mangrove trees. We saw an insect called a dragonfly. We also saw a bird called an osprey. Finally, we saw a manatee, which is a kind of mammal.

Tally Sheet

Mammals	II
Birds	III
Reptiles	III
Shellfish	I
Fish	I
Insects	I
Plants	₩ I

An Amazing Place

Our trip to the Everglades is now over. Look at our tally sheet. We've seen many different kinds of plants and animals in just three days. This huge wetland is the perfect place for many of these plants and animals to live. The Everglades really is an amazing place.

Look at our tally sheet. Did we see more plants or animals?

Tally Sheet

Mammals	II
Birds	III
Reptiles	III
Shellfish	I
Fish	I
Insects	I
Plants	ⲯ I

Glossary

fresh water   water that doesn't contain salt

habitat   a place where a plant or animal usually lives

hammock   an area of dry land within a wetland

marsh   a wetland with grasses and moving water

predator   an animal that eats other animals

swamp   a wetland that has soft, wet ground and still water

wetland   land covered or soaked with water

wilderness area   a large section of land where no people live and the animals and land are protected

Index